The Associate Minister's Bootcamp

By Rev. Karen E. Belton

Printed in the United States of America

First Printing, 2018

ISBN: 9781793257468

Published by Purpose Publishing House
PurposePublishingHouse@gmail.com
www.PurposePublishingHouse.com

TABLE OF CONTENTS

INTRODUCTION

As pastor of a small congregation, it has become increasingly apparent to me the need for dedicated, committed and faithful help in the ministry. Whether the help comes by way of lay members or called ministers of the gospel, I have personally come to the conclusion that ministry will never be a one-man or one-woman show. Having had the privilege of serving in the capacity of an executive assistant and associate to my former pastor, I thought I had seen it all and experienced the full run of ministry. However, it wasn't until I stepped into the office of pastor myself that I would understand and receive clarity of what it means to have the right kind of help.

This training has been designed to assist you, the associate minister, gain a better perspective of who you are and what your role should be in the local church. As we all know, the work of the ministry can be quite challenging, requiring everyone not only to know their role, but to operate and function properly in it. The Bible records the letter of the Apostle Paul to the church at Ephesus, wherein he states that the Lord gave the church the five-fold ministry. In Ephesians 4:11, Paul says, *"He gave some apostles, prophets, evangelists, pastors and teachers."* It is God's intention for us to work together for the sake of His kingdom.

With the harvest being plentiful, and laborers being few, it is absolutely necessary that the *few* work together in our called positions to get this work done. This is what God intended, and as such, there is no need to reinvent the wheel. There is a familiar phrase that is often used, "When you know better, you do better." Through this training, it is my goal to bring these words to life. Believing Proverbs 27:17, *"As iron sharpens iron,"* my prayer is that this time of training, instruction and fellowship brings each of us closer to the image of God's elect and chosen vessel. *~Karen E. Belton*

I

The Pastor & You: Knowing the Man or Woman You Serve

I have come to realize that there is no such thing as a part-time pastor. It matters not that he or she is not in an office at the church daily. With or without modern technology, the pastor's office is where he or she is. If asked, in most cases, pastors will say they are on the job 24/7. As you and I know, the pastor is expected to be all things to all people, and almost virtually at all times. This leaves very little time, if any, that the pastor *is not* on call. All of this can bring about extreme pressure and stress to that individual pastor. Personally, I knew pastoring would be hard, especially after assisting one for 14 years, but what I didn't know was just how hard it would be after stepping into the actual position. That's why Paul, in his letter to Timothy, concentrated on the orderliness of the leader's personality. The pastor must be well disciplined, and maintain order. It was necessary during Timothy's time, and it's necessary today. When you look at a partial list of the pastors' role, in addition to the duties the members further expect of them, you have to muster up some mercy for them. Let's take a look at the short list below:

Preach	Visit the Sick	Attend Community Meetings
Teach	Visit the Prison	Settle Disputes
Lead	Perform Weddings	Attend Court
Counsel	Officiate Funerals	Study & Meditate
Pray	Baptize	Prepare Sermons
Plan	Serve	Prepare Bible Studies

All of this for the people of God, and that's NOT all! What if the pastor is not so organized, or is a procrastinator? Then factor in the pastor's personal or family needs? As the associate, you must consider all of this and so much more. Your call, just like that of the pastor, is not to have selfishness. You, too, have been called to a life of sacrifice and service. Now where do you fit in? How do you make a difference?

I am reminded of book I read some 15 or more years ago written by Robyn Gool titled, *Every Ministry Need Help! Not Any Help, but the Right Kind of Help*. In this book, the author addresses detailed accounts of an effective Ministry of Helps that is inclusive of every ministry within the church, especially that of the leadership and the associate minister. With that, ask yourself, your pastor and even God, "Am I the right kind of help, and if not, how can I be?" The man or woman that you serve has a great need for your service. Getting to know them and their current strengths and capacities, will serve you well in assisting them to carry out the mandate and vision given them by God. Every individual in the Bible that God used to accomplish long term work had someone assigned to assist them according to their need.

My motto in ministry and in life comes directly from the Word of God, and it has served me well. *"To serve as unto the Lord."* (Colossians 3:23).

Those who diligently serve under my leadership know this. Why is that important? If you don't know your pastor's heart, you can't have your pastor's heart. This is an important point because the most effective ministries are the ones where the people have the heart of their pastor and are willing to do things his or her way, making way for the vision of that ministry to operate as God intended. So be open to getting to know your pastor's heart for the work, so that you can be a help and not a hindrance. There are several ways that you can get to know your pastor. I remember studying the way my pastor related to the members, as well as his staff. He arranged for his associates to have monthly fellowship and training with him. I paid attention to how he shared his love for God and his family. I watched and learned his preaching and teaching style. The only way I could help him was to know him and heart. I also had to know his strengths and weaknesses, not to hurt him, but to help him. I felt it was a duty as well as a privilege, because I would be helping in the work, as well as growing and maturing as a leader at the same time.

Bootcamp Lesson 101

_____

_____

_____

_____

_____

_____

_____

_____

_____

_____

_____

_____

_____

_____

_____

_____

_____

Bootcamp Lesson 101

_____

_____

_____

Bootcamp Lesson 101

_____

_____

_____

_____

_____

_____

_____

_____

_____

_____

_____

_____

_____

_____

_____

_____

_____

_____

Bootcamp Lesson 101

_____

_____

_____

_____

_____

_____

_____

_____

_____

_____

_____

_____

_____

_____

_____

_____

_____

_____

_____

_____

Bootcamp Lesson 101

_____

_____

_____

_____

_____

_____

_____

_____

_____

_____

_____

_____

_____

_____

_____

_____

_____

II

The Associate: Knowing Your Role

It's important on any job or assignment to know what is required and expected of you. When applying for most jobs, one of the first things people look for is the detailed position description. That's right! Not just the pay range, but what will be the minimum requirements needed for the person to do the job. The reality for the associate minister in most cases is that the position is not a paid one, but a called one. Even though you may not be paid, there is still a responsibility to the call of God. When God called Moses to His service to lead the children of Israel, He also called forth help for Moses in the person of Aaron. God gave clear instructions that they might understand His order for leading the people. Aaron, "the associate," was not to lead, but to assist in the leading. This seems to be a touchy area that causes a lot of problems. After all, remember (Numbers 12:6-8) Miriam and Aaron's conversation against Moses behind his back? They questioned his leadership and even said, "Doesn't God speak to us as well?" Those words have been spoken many times since the days of Moses and have caused many to fall. Don't let it be you. The goal throughout this training is to get the basic understanding of your role as an associate, and to give you a nudge in the right direction. The role one must take is that of support. It is as simple as that. You must understand that an associate is one who assists, and in this case, you are assisting the pastor in leading the church or people of God. You are positioned to be the greatest support that the pastor will have in the church or ministry. I know that every pastor has different leadership styles and models based on their personality and even character of the church they serve. As a former associate minister, I, along with the other associates, were personally trained by our pastor.

He was aware of each one of our specific areas of gifting, therefore, he used that to determine where and how we would best serve the ministry. Once we understood our role in that ministry, and we operated in it. So whatever leadership type you sit under, you are there, so go with it and honor God and the man or woman of God that you serve. Remember, "Iron Sharpens Iron," and that can be hard at times, but hang in there. You will become better through the process.

Bootcamp Lesson 102

_____

_____

_____

_____

_____

_____

_____

_____

_____

_____

_____

_____

_____

_____

_____

_____

_____

Bootcamp Lesson 102

_____

_____

_____

_____

_____

_____

_____

_____

_____

_____

_____

_____

_____

_____

_____

_____

_____

_____

_____

Bootcamp Lesson 102

_____

_____

_____

_____

_____

_____

_____

_____

_____

_____

_____

_____

_____

_____

_____

_____

_____

_____

_____

Bootcamp Lesson 102

_____

_____

_____

_____

_____

_____

_____

_____

_____

_____

_____

_____

_____

_____

_____

_____

_____

_____

_____

Bootcamp Lesson 102

_____

_____

_____

_____

_____

_____

_____

_____

_____

_____

_____

_____

_____

_____

_____

_____

_____

_____

III

Understanding Your Purpose

One of the most asked questions or concerns of Christians today, is all about purpose. What's my purpose? Why am I here? In my opinion, it all began with the *Purpose Driven Life* hype. We live in a society that will "buy-in" to anything if it's well marketed. If we spent as much time with God and meditated on His word, as we do reading books off the shelf, we would get the answer to these questions. As associates, God needs you to serve in your current capacity, as you have been given opportunity. When you know and have accepted your current, purpose fulfilling role, then you can be totally supportive of it. In other words, "Own it!"

Please realize that as the needs of the ministry changes, God's purpose for you, your gifts and abilities may change. Flexibility is a necessity!

There are a few things that I would like to cover regarding your purpose in the church or ministry that you are a part of. Keep in mind that wherever you are, God has need of you. Consider the following:

1. You may be in place temporarily to meet a specific need of the church or the pastor. Those needs can be anything from establishing a church, to establishing a ministry within that church.

2. You may be in place for training. Your time at the church is for your good. The pastor or the church may have something that you need to get to your next level. Through this experience, you may learn better how to minister to and care for God's people.

3. You may be a permanent part of the vision. If this is the case, you will always be a prevalent part of the ministry in some way.

This simply means that you are there for the long hall.

Workspace #1
Thinking It Through

Keeping in mind the three reasons of why you are planted where you are, which of the three do you feel best describes you? Explain why, and then note how you can improve in that area.

Notes:

_____

_____

_____

_____

_____

_____

_____

Bootcamp Lesson 103

_____

_____

_____

_____

_____

_____

_____

_____

_____

_____

_____

_____

_____

_____

_____

_____

_____

_____

Bootcamp Lesson 103

_____

_____

_____

_____

_____

_____

_____

_____

_____

_____

_____

_____

_____

_____

_____

_____

_____

Bootcamp Lesson 103

_____

_____

_____

_____

_____

_____

_____

_____

_____

_____

_____

_____

_____

_____

_____

_____

_____

_____

_____

_____

Bootcamp Lesson 103

_____

_____

_____

_____

_____

_____

_____

_____

_____

_____

_____

_____

_____

_____

_____

_____

_____

Bootcamp Lesson 103

_____

_____

_____

_____

_____

_____

_____

_____

_____

_____

_____

_____

_____

_____

_____

_____

_____

_____

_____

IV

The Privilege of Serving

As I have previously mentioned, God has called us to be servants. As associate ministers, you are called to serve the pastor and God's people. Being a minister is not about preaching alone. It is rather about serving and doing what needs to be done. There is no mention in the Word of God, of Jesus ever seeking glory for himself. Jesus, being the Son, and direct heir of God, never asked for special privileges or recognition. It is so important that we follow His lead. Let's not be like the disciples wrestling for position (Mark 10:35-38). They were a bit assuming, and bold in their request. So many people struggle with pride, which does nothing but hinder our growth and service. Some of us have the grand notion that we are to sit high and be served.

If a ministry is operating as it should, there is always much work to be done. I have another short list of duties I'd like to share with you. Let's call this one, "The Hit List." On this list, you will find areas of the ministry in which you can assist and serve:

Christian Education	Custodial/Janitorial Services
Hospitality Ministry	Helps Ministry
Intercessory Prayer	Transportation
Nursery/Child Care	Meals-on-Wheels
Food Pantry/Clothes Bank	Administration
Church Sports League	Mentoring/Tutoring

This is a short and possibly unconventional list for the smaller, more rural church, but there is at least one of these areas in which you, the associate can be of service, no matter the size or location of your church. I believe that if God has called you to the ministry, He will or has equipped you to operate in it. So take a second look at the list and think about where you can best serve.

Workspace #2
Is Your Service Fruitful?

It's time to think beyond the pulpit. Your most effective service will not always be confined to the four walls of a sanctuary. In the short list provided, where are you best suited to serve? Or share another area not listed. Evaluate your service on a scale of (1-5) with 5 being the highest. Explain why you gave yourself this rating.

Notes:

_____

_____

_____

_____

_____

_____

_____

_____

_____

_____

_____

_____

_____

_____

_____

_____

_____

_____

_____

_____

_____

_____

_____

_____

_____

Bootcamp Lesson 104

Bootcamp Lesson 104

_____

_____

_____

_____

_____

_____

_____

_____

_____

_____

_____

_____

_____

_____

_____

_____

_____

_____

Bootcamp Lesson 104

_____

_____

_____

_____

_____

_____

_____

_____

_____

_____

_____

_____

_____

_____

_____

_____

_____

_____

_____

Bootcamp Lesson 104

_____

_____

_____

_____

_____

_____

_____

_____

_____

_____

_____

_____

_____

_____

_____

_____

_____

_____

Bootcamp Lesson 104

_____

_____

_____

_____

_____

_____

_____

_____

_____

_____

_____

_____

_____

_____

_____

_____

_____

_____

_____

_____

V

Accountability & Faithfulness

In every area of life there should be a level of accountability and faithfulness. I cannot stress enough the importance of both these areas. It really goes back to "Serving as unto the Lord." I can honestly say that I have never worked for, or with anyone that I was not devoted to or committed to. That's called being faithful. Therefore, if you are faithful, accountability is a cake walk. It shouldn't be a labor or burden to be either accountable or faithful. Everyone in some way is subject to another. As an associate minister, you have to be accountable and faithful to God and to your pastor. Remember that position description mentioned earlier? It's how you performed those duties, that you will be evaluated. If you are given duties and assignments by your pastor, then he or she has the right to evaluate your faithfulness to fulfilling the same. The pastor, and believe it or not, the people you fellowship with, will hold you accountable for what you do, and what you don't do. Most of you know, that's a given. No matter how many things you get right, people tend to remember what you got wrong. Since you are in a position of leadership, eyes are on you, and yes, they want to know if they can count on you to come through. Your pastor and others will take note of your attendance in worship, Bible study, Sunday school, meetings and so on. Besides that, God's eyes are on you. He, like others want to know can you be trusted, so lead by example. Be faithful to your call and position. Be committed to the work. You never know who you will affect change in by getting it right. If you happen to get it wrong or miss the mark on your assignment(s), be humble enough to be the first to admit it. If not, expect your pastor to call you on it. If you are operating as God called you to, you will respectfully submit to your pastor's authority, even if you don't agree.

Workspace #3
Can I Be Trusted?

What you say and do makes a difference. Take a moment to evaluate yourself in the following areas: Dependable, Disciplined, Committed to Excellence

---

Notes:

_____

_____

_____

_____

_____

_____

_____

_____

Bootcamp Lesson 105

_____

_____

_____

_____

_____

_____

_____

_____

_____

_____

_____

_____

_____

_____

_____

_____

_____

_____

_____

Bootcamp Lesson 105

_____

_____

_____

_____

_____

_____

_____

_____

_____

_____

_____

_____

_____

_____

_____

_____

_____

_____

_____

Bootcamp Lesson 105

_____

_____

_____

_____

_____

_____

_____

_____

_____

_____

_____

_____

_____

_____

_____

_____

_____

_____

Bootcamp Lesson 105

_____

_____

_____

_____

_____

_____

_____

_____

_____

_____

_____

_____

_____

_____

_____

_____

_____

_____

Bootcamp Lesson 105

_____

_____

_____

_____

_____

_____

_____

_____

_____

_____

_____

_____

_____

_____

_____

_____

_____

_____

_____

VI

The Call to Duty: Personal & Public Responsibility

It is of great importance to God how we as ministers of the Gospel, handle our body, mind and spirit. It is important how we behave and conduct ourselves in our private, personal and public lives. Some people have the mindset that what they do in the privacy of their own home or elsewhere is just that, private. But in the word of God, Paul writes a letter recorded in **Romans 12:1-2,** *"I beseech you therefore, brethren, by the mercies of God, that ye present your bodies a living sacrifice, holy, acceptable unto God, which is your reasonable service."* God is not merely interested in your spirit, but your body as well. Your body belongs to God, and he requires us to sacrifice it constantly and/or continuously. Yes, continuously. This is not a part-time call. There should be no Clark Kent/Superman syndromes in the man or woman of God. You are in a continuous service unto the Lord, living and breathing for Him. Before you came to Christ, you lived for yourself and the world you belonged to. You thought a certain way, talked a certain way, walked a certain way, spent your money a certain way and dressed a certain way. You even ate and drank a certain way. You did things your way! No matter how good you perceived your life to be without Christ, there was immorality, drunkenness, overeating, greed, slothfulness, and so much more. Now, you have not only been saved and belong to the household of faith, but you have been CALLED to a higher standard and responsibility. For most or all of us, this responsibility can be a struggle, if truth be told, but God give us power to overcome. **2 Cor. 10:5**, "C*ast down imaginations, and every high thing that exalts itself against the knowledge of God, and bring into captivity every thought to the* *obedience of Christ."* Again, it may be a struggle, but you can do it! You have no choice. There may be things that you want to do and places you may want to go, but make the SACRIFICE necessary to do what God requires of you. You may not understand now, but God will make it plain and reveal it to you later. If you move upon a fleshly, worldly desire, it can be detrimental to you and any hope of a future in ministry. We sing the song, "I give myself away," but do you really. The lyrics go on to say, "My life is not my own, to you I belong." These words should represent the true essence of your life as a minister of the Gospel. A lot of people, especially this generation, would say that it is impossible to live this priestly life, as those who were of the biblical age. The word tells us that from everlasting to everlasting He is God. So the God the priests and prophets served in the Bible is the same God we serve today. He is looking for a *Total Commitment*! If God were to ask you the question, "Do you love me more than these?" What would be your answer?

When Jesus called the disciples to follow him, he did not give them an ultimatum. He already knew who they were, where they were from, and what they did for a living. Yet He called them. He called them into a different life and lifestyle, one of true sacrifice. Can you remember when the Lord called you into this service, this life of sacrifice for His sake? We should perform a continuous self-examination. Talk to God and inquire of Him as to if you are still pleasing Him. If you are getting it right.

Workspace #4
Thinking It Through

What are some areas of concern for your ability to live as priests today? Be honest and candid with yourself. List your pros and cons.

Notes:

_____

_____

_____

_____

_____

_____

_____

_____

_____

_____

_____

_____

_____

_____

_____

_____

_____

_____

_____

_____

_____

_____

_____

_____

_____

_____

_____

_____

_____

_____

_____

Bootcamp Lesson 106

_____

_____

_____

_____

_____

_____

_____

_____

_____

_____

_____

_____

_____

_____

_____

_____

_____

_____

Bootcamp Lesson 106

_____

_____

_____

_____

_____

_____

_____

_____

_____

_____

_____

_____

_____

_____

_____

_____

_____

_____

Bootcamp Lesson 106

_____

_____

_____

_____

_____

_____

_____

_____

_____

_____

_____

_____

_____

_____

_____

_____

_____

_____

_____

_____

Bootcamp Lesson 106

_____

_____

_____

_____

_____

_____

_____

_____

_____

_____

_____

_____

_____

_____

_____

_____

_____

_____

Bootcamp Lesson 106

_____

_____

_____

_____

_____

_____

_____

_____

_____

_____

_____

_____

_____

_____

_____

_____

_____

_____

_____

VII

When or If You Should Move On

This subject matter can be quite controversial, and most would say that it comes by way of a difference of opinion, doctrine or better yet, some sort of power struggle. There may come a time that you feel the need to move on, but as previously stated, the associate is planted where he or she is for a reason. If you know that you're there temporarily, the circumstances will line up with the spirit of the Lord. He will reveal when and if that time has come to move on. The problem usually arises when we move before the timing is right. Some of us will be so anxious to move on, that we miss God's timing. Only God knows the right time. So avoid this mistake at all costs. I have witnessed occasions when ministers were so ready to move on and do their "own thing," that they made a mess and a mockery of the ministry. If the

Lord has given you a vision for a ministry, or you are currently operating a ministry outside the church, it should not interfere with your current duties or responsibilities. Sometimes you have to humble yourself, and trust that God knows when it's your time. There is a phrase, "Drink no wine before its time." The process of making the perfect bodied wine has much to do with TIME (the aging process). If the timing is off, then all you'll have is sour grapes. If it's simpler to work and minister together, until the Lord moves you on then do so. Don't let what you hear and see others doing push or urge you to move. There will be confirmation by the Holy Spirit, just as it was in Acts 13:1-2, when they were in the church in Antioch, worshipping and fasting together, the Holy Spirit said, *"separate me Barnabas and Saul for the work that I have called you to."* The Holy Spirit confirms His PURPOSE.

Workspace #5

Assessment: Stay or Move On

Remember to pray and wait until you have a definite word from the Lord. It is easy to move on emotions, but that is not always the best way. Please continue to be honest with yourself. You and others can talk you into thinking you're doing the right thing, but if the Lord has not spoken, *Be Still*. Take a moment to really meditate and make note of your reflections.

Notes:

_____

_____

_____

_____

_____

_____

_____

Bootcamp Lesson 107

_____

_____

_____

_____

_____

_____

_____

_____

_____

_____

_____

_____

_____

_____

_____

_____

_____

_____

Bootcamp Lesson 107

_____

_____

_____

_____

_____

_____

_____

_____

_____

_____

_____

_____

_____

_____

_____

_____

_____

_____

_____

_____

Bootcamp Lesson 107

_____

_____

_____

_____

_____

_____

_____

_____

_____

_____

_____

_____

_____

_____

_____

_____

_____

_____

_____

_____

Bootcamp Lesson 107

Bootcamp Lesson 107

_____

_____

_____

_____

_____

_____

_____

_____

_____

_____

_____

_____

_____

_____

_____

_____

_____

_____

Goals: Action Plan Moving Forward

1. Get excited about your future and mark your progress (ministry & personal).
2. Set long-term and short-term goals. Write them down and make them reachable. Revisit the plan for changes when necessary.
3. Stay focused and pace yourself in whatever goals you have set.
4. Communicate regularly with your pastor and ask for guidance when needed.
5. Make sure to get an accountability partner. One that will tell you the truth.
6. Regularly spend one on one time with the Lord. (pray, meditate & study).
7. Always evaluate your actions (what worked and what didn't).

Connect with Rev. Karen E. Belton

Website: www.KarenBeltonMinistries.com

Email: MinBootCamp@gmail.com

Made in the USA
Lexington, KY
25 January 2019